PrayerStarters

In Times of Sadness or Depression

Text © 2000 by Molly Wigand
Published by One Caring Place
Abbey Press
St. Meinrad, Indiana 47577

Library of Congress Catalog Number
00-100742

ISBN 0-87029-339-7

Printed in the United States of America

PrayerStarters

In Times of Sadness or Depression

by Molly Wigand

ONE
CARING
PLACE

Abbey Press

Introduction

God created us to be happy. The beauty of nature, loving relationships, and spiritual fulfillment—all are part of the universe's magnificent plan for all God's children.

But, despite the many wonders of our world, all human beings sometimes experience sadness or depression. When our joy and peace are locked up within our hearts, we find it difficult or even impossible to find the good and benevolent in our lives and in our world.

Sometimes our depression has an identifiable trigger. Chronic illness, the loss of a loved one, financial problems, and failed relationships can make it difficult to find the beauty and joy in our world.

At other times, though, depression has a chemical or physical cause. Our bodies, for a variety of reasons, don't provide us with sufficient amounts of endorphins, the "feel-good" enzymes in our brains. Seemingly without reason, we may live in constant emotional pain and despair.

Whether our depression is caused by external events or by internal imbalance, prayer heals us and returns joy to our lives. By nurturing our spiritual nature, we replace our sadness and despair with God's love and peace. Whether we practice our spirituality in the context of organized religion or follow a more private and personal journey of faith, prayer works wonders in handling stress.

Prayer can happen in a myriad of miraculous ways. Reciting favorite Scripture passages, meditating in silence, embracing our imperfections, listening to beautiful music—each of these human moments (and many others) can connect us with our higher natures and help heal our wounded lives.

By expanding our definition of prayer to include more than verbal exchanges between our God and ourselves, we can make the simplest actions in each day living prayers. By engaging in daily life prayers, we can grow beyond our sadness and depression. By regaining our perspective, we grow to understand our emotions and renew our relationship with our spiritual selves.

Whether you read the 31 meditations in order or flip through randomly to find a message that speaks to you on a particular day, may these prayer starters comfort your heart and ease your pain as you embark on your spiritual voyage.

Sunshine and Shadows

"In a dark time, the eye begins to see,
I meet my shadow in the deepening shade;
I hear my echo in the echoing wood."
—Theodore Roethke

Throughout our lives, we all experience times of darkness and times of light. Though the joyful times are a pleasure to go through, we may wish away all sadness and depression. Without our sorrowful moments, though, we would not be fully human. Our sad times teach us about ourselves, revealing our inner reserves of resilience and strength.

PrayerStarters

What sad occurrence weighs on your heart today?

Think of a sad time you have experienced in the past. How did God's love help you through?

Dear God,
I'm feeling so sad about _____.
Help me to understand that sorrow
is part of being human. Be my guide
as I struggle to cope with my distress.

We're Only Human

*"Life is like playing a violin in public
and learning the instrument as one goes on."*
—Samuel Butler

Being human has never been an easy task. Our humanity makes us vulnerable to heartbreak, disappointment, and regret. Our expectations of ourselves, along with the expectations others have for us, can be difficult or even impossible to meet. By embracing our imperfections and limitations, we grow to accept ourselves as lovable children of God. We ease our sadness when we allow ourselves to make (and learn from) our human mistakes.

PrayerStarters

List five big mistakes you've made in your life.

_____
_____
_____

Have you forgiven yourself for being human? Can you start today?

Dear God,
My remorse and embarrassment about _____
keep me from being fully happy and fully alive.
Let your forgiveness be an example to me
as I try to forgive myself.

Without a Word

"Prayer is not asking.
It is a longing of the soul."
—Mohandas Gandhi

Sometimes it's impossible to verbalize the reasons for our sadness. Vague, melancholy feelings may cast our hearts into the darkness of confusion. Without our saying a word, God understands and accepts the changing landscape of human moods and emotions. God listens to every silent soul prayer with empathy and love.

PrayerStarters

Set aside a silent morning. Whether at home in a quiet room or alone in nature, contemplate the sadness and depression you feel. Allow God to listen to your unspoken questions and needs. Listen for God's wise and loving response in the silence that surrounds you.

God's Promise of Renewal

*"For I will restore health to you,
and your wounds I will heal."*
—Jeremiah 30:17

Physicians, psychologists, and theologians agree that strong connections exist among our minds, our bodies, and our spirits. Feeling depressed can affect one's physical health in many ways. When you're depressed, you may experience extreme fatigue, or you may have difficulty sleeping at night. Depression affects one's appetite and inner rhythms. When we ask God to heal us, we can be assured that our bodies, minds, and souls will be made whole.

PrayerStarters

My body needs healing. My mind and soul need healing, too. I welcome the blessings of _____ into my daily life.

Dear God,
Help me understand the connection
among my mind, body, and spirit.
Bring joy back to my life.
Make me healthy and whole.

Don't Look Back

"Even God cannot change the past."
—Agathon

Unresolved guilt and remorse can cause depression in our lives. And once depression takes hold, it's difficult to find the serenity to forgive ourselves and move on. God understands our humanity and knows that our journeys through life will be sprinkled with mistakes and misjudgments. Prayer reconnects us with God's message of forgiveness, acceptance, and love. Prayer gives us the strength and hope to begin anew.

PrayerStarters

I feel guilty about _____
_____.

I can make amends by _____
_____.

Dear God,
Grant me serenity as I move forward in my life. Help me to be patient with the person I was yesterday, as I vow to make the most of today and face tomorrow with hope and courage.

Miracles Within Us

*"The ladder that leads to the kingdom
is hidden within your soul...
Dive into yourself,
and in your soul you will discover
the stairs by which to ascend."*
—Saint Isacc of Nineveh

We often underestimate the reserves of strength and insight we possess. God's power and wisdom live within our hearts. It takes courage to dive into our souls and examine the issues and troubles that cause sadness to overpower us. When we take time to still our minds and look within, we find that God has provided us with built-in answers to our questions and relief from our pain.

PrayerStarters

My inner voice has been telling me to _____
_____.

Other voices have been saying _____
_____.

Which voice will you listen to?

Dear God,
Help me to trust the voices of hope and possibility within me. Remind me to pay attention to your spirit in my
heart and mind.

God Bless Friends

*"A friend is the one who comes in
when the whole world has gone out."*
—Alban Goodier

Depression isolates us from those who care. When we're feeling low, we hesitate to bring others down by sharing our heartaches. Even when others reach out to us and offer their support, we may feel unworthy of their friendship. God blesses us by placing sensitive, giving people in our lives to help us through times of sadness and despair. When someone extends the hand of friendship, we are worthy to accept the gesture with gratitude and grace.

PrayerStarters

Today I will reach out to _____ in trust
and friendship. I will share my sadness and fears about
_____.

Dear God,
Give me the courage to show my shadow side
to friends and family. Help me hear their
responses of acceptance and love.

Tiny Treasures

"For in the dew of little things the heart finds its morning and is refreshed."
—Kahlil Gibran, *The Prophet*

Even when confusion, sadness, and despair touch our lives, the world's small miracles glimmer with hope. The shimmer of moonlight on a calm, clear lake, the feathery down on a baby bird, the taste of wild strawberries, the fragrance of a rosebud—these and other blessings of nature give us little reasons to smile. We can make a conscious effort to open our senses and our hearts and discover the joys of God's creation.

PrayerStarters

My favorite taste is _____.
My favorite sight is _____.
My favorite sound is _____.
My favorite smell is _____.
My favorite sensation is _____.

Dear God,
May the gift of my five senses
lift me from depression to joy.

Feel God's Touch

"In the circle of earthly existence
You shine so finely,
it surpasses understanding.
God hugs you.
You are encircled by the arms
of the mystery of God."
—Hildegard of Bingen

The caring touch of another person helps heal our sorrows. A caring hug, a pat on the back, or a soothing hand eases our pain and reminds us that we are not alone. When sadness comes and you are alone, visualize and imagine the touch of God's nurturing hand.

Likewise, share your gentle touch with others who carry a heavy load. Every little gesture of kindness makes our world a more loving place.

PrayerStarters

I could use a hug from _____.
_____ could probably use a hug from me.

Dear God,
Teach me to share your love
with hugs and gentle touches.
Help me to feel your love
in the kind gestures of others.

Remember—It's All Good

*"Love all Creation
The whole of it and every grain of sand...
Love everything."*
—Fyodor Dostoyevsky

When depression clouds our vision, we find it difficult to find the good in others. When we feel unworthy and unloved, it's tempting to focus on the faults of others. However, with some effort and prayer, it is possible to make love a habit.

God's unconditional love is a model of how we should regard our fellow creatures. Our own sadness and depression give us insights into the pain and grief accompanying our friends and family members on their journeys. Pray for love and understanding. In loving others, your sorrows will be eased.

PrayerStarters

_____ is getting on my nerves.
With God's help, I can focus on this person's
wonderful traits, such as _____.
I can accept and embrace this person,
even the traits that annoy or trouble me.

Dear Lord,
Give me the wisdom to extend
to those I meet
patience, acceptance, and understanding.
Likewise, bless me with the gift
of patient, accepting, understanding friends.

The World Is On Your Side

*"You will go out in joy
and be led forth in peace;
the mountains and hills before you
will burst into song,
and all the trees of the field
will clap their hands."*

—Isaiah 55:12

    God's assurances have sustained the world for thousands of years. In times of sadness, keep your Bible nearby. Allow the timeless stories, psalms, songs, and prayers to enter your mind and heart, easing your pain.

    Attending religious services can also take away our feelings of isolation and loneliness. By joining in a community of worship and prayer, our connections to God and humankind are enriched and strengthened.

PrayerStarters

I will commit myself to a new spiritual ritual: _____

_____.

I will take the time each week to read my favorite
Bible verses:_____.

Dear God,
Keep me mindful of the spiritual wealth
to be found in the Bible and in my religious
community. Help me stay connected with
the spiritual resources in my life.

Horizons of Hope

"This grand show is eternal.
It is always sunrise somewhere..."
—John Muir

People considered it revolutionary when early astronomers maintained that the earth was not the center of the universe. When we're depressed, we sometimes lose sight of that discovery. We tend to focus tightly on our own problems, making ourselves the center of our attention.

If we keep the warm sunshine of God's love at the center of our spiritual universe, our problems and sadness seem less overwhelming. Keep your eyes on the horizon and realize that, before long, a beautiful new day will dawn. Believe that tomorrow will be more manageable than today.

PrayerStarters

Here's something good that might happen tomorrow: _____.

Here's a problem I can focus on outside myself: ____
_____.

Here's what I can do to help: _____
_____.

The Bold Believer

*"Sometimes I've believed as many
as six impossible things before breakfast."*
—Lewis Carroll, *Alice in Wonderland*

In these logical times, we may be tempted to explain away everyday miracles by quoting scientific principles and mathematical probabilities. But by daring to believe in God's wondrous plan, we renew our child-like sense of awe. We can find miracles in a refreshing glass of ice water, in the synchronicity of our body's living cells, and in the music of birds outside our window.

When we are depressed, it may feel as though we'll never feel happy again. What a miracle it is every time we're touched by God's emotional healing and our sadness gives way to optimism and hope.

PrayerStarters

Look out the window. Describe what you see.

_____
_____

What miracles can you witness right this very minute?_____
_____

Keep on Striving

*"Ah, but a man's reach should exceed his grasp,
or what's a heaven for?"*
—Robert Browning

Depression creates a feeling of hopelessness.
Despair can paralyze us, making us feel trapped in
unhealthy and unhappy situations. Relief from this helplessness is always just a prayer away.

With God's help we can overcome our circumstances and find a happy and productive life on earth.
Whether we feel stuck in a tedious job, a difficult relationship, or simply have lost touch with our optimism,
God gives us the strength to continue reaching for the
stars and striving for happiness.

PrayerStarters

My most daring dream is that I _____
_____.

    One thing I can do today to move toward the fulfill-
ment of my dream is_____
_____.

Dear God,
Help me to realize
that my dreams can come true.
Show me the steps I can take
each and every day
to bring me closer to my goal.

Fruits of the Spirit

*"Take hold of the life
that really is life."*
—1 Timothy 6:19

Depression can be a painful and long-lasting by-product of grief and loss. When you lose someone you love, it may feel as if you have a "hole in our soul." It can feel difficult to remain grounded in your faith when sorrow overcomes your daily life.

God can help us reconnect with our spiritual life. When we're spiritually sound, we are able to believe God's promise that death is but a passage to another, more beautiful realm. In time, God's love eases our pain and allows us to remember our loved one with joy and thankfulness.

PrayerStarters

I miss the company of _____.

A favorite memory of this person is _____
_____
_____.

Dear God,
Help me to let go of my sadness
and release _____ to
your eternal care. Help me to
reconnect with the joy and beauty
of _____'s remarkable life.

Look to the Light

*"The eye is the lamp of the body.
So, if your eye is healthy,
your whole body will be full of light."*
—Matthew 6:22

As humans, we choose how we view our circumstances. God has given us the freedom to "see the glass as half empty or half full."

Depression clouds our vision, blinding us to the goodness that surrounds us. In prayer, we can ask God to reopen our eyes to the blessings in our world. With God's help, we can rediscover the hidden joy in each moment of our lives. We can feel glad and grateful for every breath we take.

PrayerStarters

Close your eyes and visualize yourself in a happy, contented place. Describe your surroundings:

_____

_____

What can you do to make your real life more like your visualization? _____

_____

Dear God,
Help me to see the best
in everyone and everything
around me.

Pray for Everybody

*"May suffering ones be suffering free
And the fear struck fearless be.
May the grieving shed all grief
And the sick find health relief."*

—Zen chant

Medical researchers have found evidence that healing is accelerated and enhanced when others pray for a patient's recovery. By asking others to pray for you, your depression or sadness may be relieved more quickly and completely.

Likewise, others who struggle with physical or psychological illnesses need your prayers. Praying for others moves the focus from our own difficulties to the lives and struggles of all our fellow humans.

PrayerStarters

    I will ask _____ to pray for me in my time of sorrow.

    I will include _____ in my daily prayers as well.

Dear God,
Help me to see the power
in a community
of prayer and meditation.
Keep me and those I love
close to you in hope and faith.

Love Your
Neighbor *And* Yourself

*"Love means to love that which is unlovable,
or it is no virtue at all:"*
—G.K. Chesterton

Depression and sadness sometimes propels us into a downward spiral of spiritual emptiness and personal shame. Even though our depression is rooted in physical and psychological causes, we may actually feel guilty for feeling depressed.

God understands and accepts us, even at our lowest points. We can learn to forgive ourselves and others for our changing moods and feelings, acknowledging that every emotion we experience is part of the complex and multi-textured canvas of humanity.

PrayerStarters

Find a picture of yourself as a child. See the innate worth and beauty showing in your innocent smile. Find the child-like, innocent place within you. Believe that you still possess the magic and wonder of childhood.

Dear God,
Help me to remember
that I am your good and worthy child.
Remind me to embrace your world
with childlike enthusiasm and grace.

Not Seeing Is Believing!

"Hold on to my hand
even when I am gone away from you."
—Pueblo verse

In times of depression, it often feels as though everyone, even God, has abandoned us. Drowning in despair, we may long to see an earthly sign of God's love and commitment to us.

But the miracle of faith happens only when we can believe without seeing. When we sink into the mire of sadness, we can reach out in confidence for God's all-powerful hand. God rescues us from depression. Through childlike faith we realize that all the love and joy in the universe are on our side as we strive to become whole again.

PrayerStarters

Make room for God in your home.
Set a place at the table.

Imagine God in a chair beside you
as you work and play.

Have a conversation with God,
your faithful friend.

Know that the divine presence
is powerful and real.

Blessings In Disguise

"Life is so generous a giver, but we, judging its gifts by their covering, cast them away as ugly or heavy or hard. Remove the covering, and you will find beneath it a living splendor, woven of love, by wisdom, with power."
—Fra Giovanni

Sometimes the things we regard as misfortunes are actually valuable life gifts from God. Think of a stormy day. Clouds gather, the sky darkens, and the world has a gloomy pallor. But the storm provides needed moisture for all living things.

Similarly, unfortunate events may be the gentle rain we need to transform our lives into something even better. Our despair is transformed into meaning as we grow and flourish according to God's plan.

PrayerStarters

What lessons might God be teaching you through your emotional and physical distress? _____
_____
_____

If, with God's help, you change your life, how will things be different?_____
_____

Dear God,
Help me to see the lessons
in the ups and downs of my earthly life.

Happy To Be Here

"Eat your bread with joy,
drink your wine with a merry heart."
—Ecclesiastes 9:7

Depression and sadness make it difficult to appreciate the ways God provides for our most basic survival. While our lives may not be perfect, and though our pain is real, we are fortunate to have the food and shelter we need to get by.

Beyond mere survival, God provides our senses with the savory warmth of fresh-baked bread, the juicy richness of a ripe, red apple, and the restorative refreshment of ice water. By focusing on the blessings we enjoy rather than the inadequacies we see in our lives, we develop an attitude of gratitude and joy.

PrayerStarters

Contemplate the bountiful material blessings you enjoy every day.

What small heavenly gifts are you taking for granted?

_____

_____

Thank God for your favorite things. Show your gratitude by sharing your bounty with those who have less.

Time Is On Our Side

*"Do you have the patience to wait
till your mind settles and the water is clear?"*
—Tao Te Ching

"Give me patience and give me it now!" Patience eludes us when we're waiting for clarity and healing in our lives. As with our physical bodies, though, healing our minds and spirits takes time.

When we trust in God's timetable for our lives, we receive the blessing of patience along with the healing and wholeness we desperately crave. Like the angle of sunlight through a kitchen window, our perspective changes with the passage of time. If we have the patience to wait and see, our shadows of sadness are transformed into pools of joy and light.

PrayerStarters

Take a ride in the car. Find the generosity to accept and affirm the rights of other travelers. Think of red lights as opportunities for reflection and meditation. Consider slow traffic an exercise in mindful patience and love.

What other "waiting times" can become opportunities for mindfulness?_____

Hold a Good Thought

"Life consists
in what a man
is thinking of all day."
—Ralph Waldo Emerson

We have the responsibility to choose the images and messages that color our thoughts every day. If depression and sadness darken our lives, we can choose to eliminate many negative, violent, and troubling stimuli from our homes. By mindfully selecting our music, movies, television, and reading material, we create an environment conducive to healing and joy. When we surround ourselves with positive input, we discourage negativity from poisoning our hearts and minds.

PrayerStarters

Enforce a one-week media fast. Listen to no news or movies. Read no magazines. Turn off the car radio. Rediscover quiet solitude and uncluttered human interaction. Experience the healing power of silence.

Dear God,
Thank you for the chance
to turn down the volume
on the noise and clamor in the world.
Help me listen for your voice
in the silent spaces of my days.

The Power of Good

*"I believe that unarmed truth
and unconditional love
will have the final word."*
—Martin Luther King, Jr.

Our personal sadness and depression may be deepened by our sense of helplessness in the face of disturbing world events. Watching and reading news of war, famine, and violence may intensify our feelings of despair.

One solution is to pray for peace and prosperity for all. Dare to believe that God's love and truth will prevail. Focus on stories of love and concern in action. Know that your actions in your own neighborhood and home are blessings that make a positive difference in the world.

PrayerStarters

What world event troubles you right this minute?

_____

Visualize a peaceful and serene outcome for this world event.

Believe in the power of prayer.
Pray for world leaders.
Pray for powerless victims.
Pray for the poor.
Pray for the hungry.
Pray for peace.

Love—A Two-Way Street

*"There is no greater invitation to love
than loving first."*
—St. Augustine of Hippo

When depression strikes, the unworthiness we feel may make us withdraw from others—even our closest friends and family. Try to remember that love is the most powerful antidote to depression and despair. By showing our care and concern to those around us, we open our hearts to the love that is ours in return.

God's love touches our lives even during our darkest hours. Visualize the power of love to ease our pain and comfort our souls.

PrayerStarters

Think of a friend or family member who means the world to you. Write an "I love you" note. List the many ways your life has been touched and blessed by this person's love and concern.

Dear God,
Don't let me go another day without expressing my love to _____. Give me the courage and eloquence to say exactly what I feel.

Good Grief!

"Accept suffering.
It can stretch your heart
to make room
for greater love and joy."
—Lisa Engelhardt, *Acceptance Therapy*

Remind yourself: By the grace of God, you will someday feel better. Hope will be restored. Joy will return to your heart. You will laugh and smile and love again.

When your sadness and depression depart at last, preparing your heart and soul for peace and well being, you'll feel more grateful than ever for God's loving, healing touch. As you experience your returning joy, vow to be an understanding listener and friend to those in emotional need.

PrayerStarters

The first thing I'm going to do when I feel better is

_____.

What is stopping me from doing this right now?

_____

_____

Dear God,
Help me do everything I can
to emerge from my cocoon of sadness.
Never let me forget
that a brighter day is coming.

Small Is Beautiful

"How small
it's all."
—James Joyce, *Finnegan's Wake*

Take an imaginary trip to the moon. Look back at the beautiful blue planet you've left behind. Try to locate your continent, your country, your state, and your town. See if you can pinpoint your home.

In the whole context of your life, in the vast array of earthly experience, how significant is the sadness you feel today? Consider the unlimited heavenly resources available to you and to all human beings dealing with trouble and turmoil. Discover hope in the reality of God's plan for the universe.

PrayerStarters

On a quiet, clear, starry night, look up in the sky. Silently contemplate the enormity of the universe.

Here are five problems that are bigger than mine:

1. _____
2. _____
3. _____
4. _____
5. _____

Dear God,
Help me keep things in perspective.

It's All Good

"I accept heartily and gratefully
what Nature has done for me,
and I am pleased with myself....
Being all good,
he has made things all good."
—Montaigne

Depression often springs from feelings of inadequacy, the sense that we are less than we should be in the eyes of God. We may feel we're not smart enough, thin enough, tough enough, beautiful enough, or perfect enough to merit God's love.

God's grace assures us that we are loved because of who we are. God made us human and loves us that way. We should love us, too.

PrayerStarters

Here are three really good things about me:

_____ _____ _____

Here are three really good things about being human:

_____ _____ _____

Dear God,
Thank you
for making me this way...
a one-of-a-kind,
imperfect-but-lovable
human being.

God Cries With Us

*"Blessed are you now,
right this minute,
while you are suffering."*
—Albert Schweitzer

God is not a judgmental parent who scolds us to cheer up and look on the bright side. Through God's humanity, every emotion—negative or positive—is understood and accepted. You never have to "put on a happy face" for God.

Cry out honestly. Weep silently. God knows what you need. Heaven will provide.

PrayerStarters

Here's how I look when I'm feeling sad or depressed:

_____

Here's how I look when I'm feeling happy:

_____

Dear God,
Thank you for understanding
and accepting the depths of my sorrow.
I know you have the power
to restore joy to my heart.

The Power of Imagination

"Music has charms to soothe a savage breast,
To soften rocks, or bend a knotted oak."
—William Congreve

The arts—music, painting, sculpture, dance, and literature—can heal our sorrows and ease our pain. The most powerful of all artistic endeavors are those born out of their creators' earthly experience. Attending a concert, visiting a museum, or reading a good book can lift us above our earthly trials and connect us with what it means to be a human being.

Creating our own works of art enables us to express and release feelings that may be causing us distress. Whether our medium is paint, clay, flowers, bread, or poetry, every single imaginative act restores our hope and diminishes our sadness.

PrayerStarters

Play some beautiful classical music. Imagine the human experience behind the composer's creation of this piece of music. Write a poem or story conveying the emotion you feel and hear.

Dear God,
Thank you for painters,
for composers, for authors,
for poets, for dancers,
for musicians,
and all other artists
who bring joy to our hearts
and beauty to our lives.

Tomorrow Is a Brand New Day

"Weeping may endure for a night,
but joy comes in the morning."

—Psalm 30:5

The Bible and other holy texts are peppered with stories of men and women who struggled with the emotions of sadness and despair. These people of faith had the courage to endure their emotional upheaval, knowing that God would provide.

As we see in the cycles of the seasons, the growth of plants, and the passage of days and nights on our planet, times of light and warmth follow the night and winters of our souls. Even in our darkest hours, we can believe God's promise of rebirth, renewal, and returning joy.

PrayerStarters

At bedtime, write about the struggles of the past day. Describe your sorrows. Pray for sleep to ease your sadness._____

_____

First thing in the morning, express your hopes for the day. Thank God for new beginnings. Ask for strength and guidance for the coming day._____

_____

_____

About the Author

Molly Wigand lives in suburban Kansas City with her husband and three sons. She is a contributing author for many Abbey Press products, including the book, *PrayerStarters to Help You Handle Stress*.

PrayerStarters Series

- *PrayerStarters for Dealing With Anger.* #20099
- *PrayerStarters When You're Worried.* #20098
- *PrayerStarters on the Way to Forgiveness.* #20101
- *PrayerStarters in Times of Sadness or Depression.* #20100
- *PrayerStarters in Times of Pain or Illness.* #20110
- *PrayerStarters to Help You Handle Stress.* #20107
- *PrayerStarters for Busy People.* #20109
- *PrayerStarters to Help You Heal After Loss.* #20108

Available at your favorite bookstore or gift shop, or directly from:
One Caring Place, Abbey Press,
St. Meinrad, IN 47577
(800) 325-2511
www.onecaringplace.com